GREAT TRACTOR BUILDERS

FORDSON

Ian Allan

60th

ANNIVERSARY

First published 2002

ISBN 0 7110 2828 1

Design concept and layout
© Stephen Thompson Associates 2002

Published by Ian Allan Publishing

an imprint of Ian Allan Publishing Ltd,
Hersham, Surrey, KT12 4RG

Printed by Ian Allan Printing Ltd,
Hersham, Surrey, KT12 4RG

Code 0206/C

*Picture on previous page: The last of the all British
models, the Super Dexta.*

*Opposite page: Fordsons at war, derelict building
land being ploughed up by two orange liveried model
N standard agricultural tractors in East Sussex during
late 1940.*

CONTENTS

Chapter 1   HENRY FORD –
              TRACTOR PIONEER   6 - 13

Chapter 2   IRISH INTERLUDE 1929-32   14 - 17

Chapter 3   DAGENHAM DELIGHTS
              1933-39   18 - 29

Chapter 4   TRACTORS FOR HARRY
              FERGUSON   30 - 35

Chapter 5   A MAJOR MANIFESTATION
              1945-1952   36 - 49

Chapter 6   DIESELS FOR ALL
              1952-1964   50 - 67

Chapter 7   AMERICAN DEVELOPMENTS
              1952-1963   68 -75

              SERIAL NUMBERS   76 - 77

              GLOSSARY   78 - 79

              FURTHER READING   80

INTRODUCTION

A 1940 Model N land utility model working with an Allis Chalmers All Crop Combine Harvester.

Of all the organisations which built tractors during the course of the last century, perhaps Fordson is the name most associated with the mechanisation of farming in that era. Surprisingly, it was the fortunes of war which had the most impact on the development of Fordson tractors. It was the sword rather than the plough share which, in both the 1914-18 and 1939-45 conflicts, drove forward the mechanisation of agriculture. The tractor originally produced in 1917 went on to achieve a production record of three quarters of a million units in the next ten years or so. Rugged and simple, it continued, in a modified form, as the famous Model N. In the early 1940s, it again reached new production heights when over 100 a day rolled out of the Dagenham plant.

The needs of a postwar world brought us first the 'High' Major E27N and later the famous 'New' Major and its successors, the Power Major and the Super Major. By this time the Fordson tractor was very much an institution, a virtual part of the British landscape.

A different line of development took place across the Atlantic where Ford tractor production from 1939-45 had been influenced by Henry Ford's partnership with Harry Ferguson. Later models, such as the 8N and NAA came from that lineage as did their British cousin, the Dexta.

The globalisation of the motor industry in the 1960s brought an end to the different model ranges in America and Britain. This period saw the introduction of a 'Worldwide' range with many features inherited from the US line. It is that range to which the present day New Holland models are successors.

In my view the single most significant contribution to modern agricultural mechanisation must be attributed to the 1952 Fordson Major which was the tractor that really moved farmers away from spark ignition and TVO to compression ignition and the diesel engine. Whilst the pre-1952 models had all but gone by the mid-1960s, except for those saved by the embryonic tractor preservation movement, the fact that the 'New' Major, half a century on, still finds commercial use in diverse places, has something to say for the place which Ford and Fordson have in our social, economic and agricultural history.

ACKNOWLEDGEMENTS

The author would like to thank the following for their assistance with information and illustrations for this book; David Bate, the late Charles Cawood, John Melloy, Bob Moorhouse, the Ford Motor Company's Tractor Division (now New Holland), Andrew Morland, David and Joyce Symington and all those Fordson owners with whom I have corresponded and spoken over the years. Thanks are also due to the late George Walker, formerly of Fryers of Uttoxeter in Staffordshire, and Jimmy Anderson, formerly of Frews of Perth in Scotland, who were kind enough to dispose of all their redundant service literature in my direction. They also helped to stimulate my interest in Fordson tractors which ultimately led to several books on the subject, including this one.

Contrasts in the style of literature used to promote tractors. Above: a mid 1930s advertisement and below: the cover of the Dexta promotional brochure.

HENRY FORD – TRACTOR PIONEER

This early Ford tractor used a Model B car engine and other parts from the Model K car. It was called the Automobile Plow.

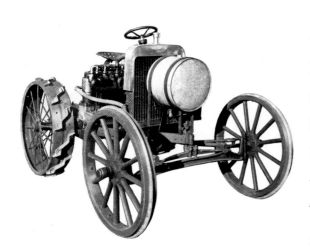

As the design developed, a radiator was added.

Henry Ford came from an agricultural background and always remembered this, but it was not until the age of 44, in 1907, that he assembled his first tractor. This was the Automobile Plow, using a 1905 Model B car engine, and other B and K car parts. At this stage the Ford Motor Company had no interest, financial or otherwise, in the project. In September 1908 the famous Model T car was introduced. It was not long before Model T parts were being used to assemble experimental tractors. A number of different designs were produced using these parts. These designs expressed Henry Ford's considered opinion that any tractor ought to have a frame to support the engine and transmission.

Then in 1914, one Eugene Farkas, who had been working in Ford's experimental department on a project to develop an electric car, was transferred to tractor design work.

Farkas was a pattern maker by trade, and first discussed the possibility of a frameless tractor with Henry Ford in 1915. Charles Sorensen was also involved and he helped Farkas to develop this concept.

Thus the tractor began to take shape. A new, larger engine, made by Hercules, was supplied for the first experimental tractors, although one version of the design was prepared which envisaged the use of a Model T engine. The transmission on the Model T prototypes had used a double reduction rear axle. By using a worm drive the necessity of this double reduction was removed. It is strange that this idea disappeared at this stage, only to reappear in the English built E27N in 1945, although by that time the needs of agriculture dictated a tractor which had to do a somewhat different job to that required in 1915-17.

Prototypes

The first prototype used a three unit construction, with engine, gearbox and rear axle joined together by flanges. The worm wheel was also at the top, requiring special lubrication arrangements if the rear axle was not to overheat.

During the process of development, it was suggested that the two halves of the rear axle could be combined. By altering the patterns, the gearbox and rear axle casings were made one.

There were probably six prototypes built to the foregoing style, each with small improvements. It is now that we have to move to look at events on the world stage to understand how the final tractors got into production.

By 1915 the experimental models containing many Model T parts, were at work.

Whilst this development work was going on in the United States, the war in Europe had produced an urgent need for alternative means of cultivating the land in Great Britain. Percival Perry, head of Ford in the United Kingdom, had approached Henry Ford to see if production of the new tractor could be started in England, sponsored by the government. Two of the early prototypes had been tried in England with success. These were in fact the Ministry of Munitions (MoM) models. This name was incorrectly applied to the later production batch of 6,000 tractors built in Britain.

Charles Sorensen had actually been dispatched to England in May 1917 to set up production of the Ford tractor in the United Kingdom. However, the German Zeppelin air raids on London caused the government contracts for tractor parts to be cancelled in

HENRY FORD

Henry Ford was born at Greenfield, Michigan, on 30th July 1863. He began to work when a boy at an engineering shop at Detroit. He rose to be chief engineer at the Edison Illumination Company and in 1903 founded a business of his own in Detroit. This became the Ford Motor Company and under his presidency rose to be the largest manufacturer of automobiles in the world, turning out 3,000 a day, and employing 50,000 workers.

In 1914 he instituted a scheme of profit-sharing for his employees, and as regards wages and hours of labour, his firm was always most liberal. In 1915 Ford brought a party of Americans to Europe in the hope of ending the Great War, but later he became convinced of the futility of this policy. When his country became a belligerent, he placed the resources of his company at its disposal and produced war materiel on a vast scale. He also subscribed $1,000,000 to the USA Liberty Loan. In December 1918, he announced his intention of retiring in favour of his son and began to develop other interests including a weekly periodical, *The Dearborn Independent*.

His first involvement with Harry Ferguson came in 1920 when a demonstration of the Ferguson plough at Dearborn brought the two men together.

Ford, whilst impressed with the plough, looked on Ferguson as a mere tractor salesman, and even got Sorenson, one of Ford's assistants, to offer him a job. What Ferguson really wanted was for Henry Ford to make his plough for him but as Ferguson had refused the offer of employment, he was advised to seek other facilities for the its manufacture. Henry Ford was of course later a participant together with Ferguson in the famous 'Handshake Agreement' which enabled Ferguson tractors to be built by Ford in the USA.

The ending of tractor production in the USA in 1928 had always upset Ford, so it was no surprise that he later set about reviving it. He was 76 by the time the 9N started to roll off the production line. He was still active enough to keep full control of the vast organisation as the world was again plunged into war in 1939. Sadly, his son Edsel died on 26th May 1943 and grandson Henry Ford II was released from the US Navy to return to the service of the company in August 1943.

On 23rd January 1944 Henry Ford II was elected executive vice-president of the Ford Motor Company and became its president on 21st September 1945, by which time Henry had stepped back and retired to Fair Lane, his country residence. After suffering a stroke he later died on 7th April 1947. He was always fascinated by engineering history and built up an incredible collection of artifacts which can still be seen today at his birth place, Greenfield Village.

Henry Ford, on the left in the bowler hat, inspects one of the final pre-production tractors.

favour of building fighter planes and an approach was made to Henry Ford to build the tractors in the USA.

The design as it stood at that stage had certain weaknesses. These were put right in a further series of prototypes often called the X series. The cooling system was inadequate so a much bigger radiator was fitted, which incorporated a cast iron top tank. To simplify the cooling system, the water pump was dispensed with.

The Model T form of low tension ignition was adopted as being more cost effective. The rear axle tended to overheat, and so the whole ensemble was turned top to bottom, putting the worm in the oil. Underslung worms however tend to aid front end rearing though this was in part overcome by the

A restored example of one of
the Fordsons shipped to Britain
in 1918 to help with the war
effort.

Another somewhat later
example with plain radiator
sides.

need to fit a heavier front axle, and of course the heavier radiator. To increase ground clearance larger wheels were fitted, 42in in diameter as opposed to the 36in of the earlier prototypes.

We have knowledge of at least nine X series tractors which were produced. The design was developed and modified through these machines, so that by the time the next models, designated X10 to X15 came along, these were very close to the first production tractors.

Here we digress again to consider what is in a name. In the United Kingdom all Ford built tractors are considered as being Fordsons whether they were part of the first 6,000 shipped over to England or not! The prototypes and the early imports did not sport the name Fordson on them at all. There was no difference between these machines and later tractors which bore the name and they should certainly not be referred to as MoM tractors. The Ministry was responsible only for the two early prototypes tried out in Britain.

The fact is that the first tractors built were not to be sold commercially, and although the company set up to build them, Henry Ford & Son, might eventually need to find a name for the tractor, especially if it ever was to be sold on the open market, the imperative of getting the first shipments to England came before this.

It has been suggested that Henry Ford had not really wanted to go into production until the tractor had been fully tried out. If this was the case, his wishes in this respect were overtaken by events. The first tractors were a success, and as production outstripped the means of shipping them to England in the convoys, it was natural that other markets would be sought for it.

On General Sale

The first tractors sold in the USA and Canada were indeed the selfsame ones as were being shipped to England without any name on, or with Henry Ford & Son stencilled on the radiator. The name Fordson first appeared around April 1919. As the number of tractors being produced built up and were being sold domestically, certain minor changes became apparent on various components. By the time the first tractors were at work in England, the name Fordson had come into use, and this is what they were all called in retrospect.

The early tractors had components supplied by many outside firms. Holley supplied manifolds, Hercules the engines, Cleveland the worm drive and gearbox components came from Timken.

The initial intention had been to produce a run of 6,000 tractors for the specific British wartime requirement. Now it is a different matter to tool up for 6,000 units and then have to produce hundreds of thousands. Indeed, nearly three quarters of a million Fordsons were built by 1928!

It is for this reason that as production got into full swing, the sourcing of components evolved until a standard pattern emerged. Experience provides for better ways of doing things, and this is where the Ford policy of continuous improvement came in.

As examples of this, early tractors had Hercules engines with rear oil fillers. These soon disappeared as did radiator side ladders. Other alterations were made as time passed. The Holley 235 Vaporiser was superseded by the 280 type in 1921 which in turn gave way to the Holley 295 in 1925. A Kingston vaporiser unit was used from 1924-26. The 12-spoke rear wheels gave way to 14-spoke from 1919, and the separate tank used to hold the petrol to start the engine, was replaced by a two-compartment main tank from 1925. Fenders became optional from 1924, and these changed to a tapered design for the rear fender from 1927 to the end of production. In 1925 the tractor was advertised at a cost of $495; delivery from the Detroit factory was extra, as were the fenders and pulley. The transmission was subject to improvement, and a transmission brake was fitted to the reverse idler from 1923. There were only three stationary and two driven plates on this assembly.

The tractor was becoming dated by 1928. It still had features which were by now outdated such as the low tension flywheel magneto, a trembler coil ignition, water air washer and an ungoverned engine.

Although we have illustrated some of the many modifications and adaptations made to the Model F as the 1917-28 tractors have now become known, it is impossible to show the hundreds of accessories and bolt-on extras that were on the market for these machines. Among the parts offered for use on the Model F were chain and shaft driven magnetos, governors, improved vaporisers and alternative transmissions.

End Of Production

The reasons for the demise of the Model F are complex. Henry Ford liked to have as much control as possible over the sales and service of his machines. In the USA most tractors were sold through Ford car dealerships. Henry Ford was not keen to supply agricultural dealers direct, or give additional discounts to enable his car dealers to re-sell tractors to such dealers and industrial convertors. Rather than give into demands by the Ford Dealers' Association, he announced that the tractor would be discontinued from the end of 1927, though in fact a few were built in 1928.

It has to be remembered that there were now many other models of tractor on the market in the USA, and Ford often made very little money on the production of his tractor. The slow-down in the US economy which was to lead to the Great Depression was starting to have a detrimental effect on car sales, and in 1927 the whole Ford plant was closed to re-tool for a new car, the Model A. It was clear that tractors were taking second place.

From its first introduction in 1918 the tractor had more impact on agricultural mechanisation than any other yet produced. It was sold in the 1920s at prices with which nobody else could compete and was copied by all and sundry, some with success and others with failure. The design of the machine was not overshadowed until the arrival of the 9N in 1939.

Before leaving the Model F, it is worth noting that a version of it was also produced in the Soviet Union. The original assembly plant was crude to say the least, and without the benefit of western technology, the early tractors wore out very quickly. Later, Ford became involved with production of these units at the Krasny Putilowitz factory. Production started in October 1924 and continued until April 1932 by which time some 50,000 units had been assembled.

Other manufacturers tried to jump on the bandwagon in copying the Fordson, but all met with limited success. General Motors offered the Samson, but this failed to make a significant impact in the huge market which Ford had opened. It was not until the Fordson's design features became outdated when compared with what other agricultural machinery manufacturers were offering in the way of tractors that the real threat appeared, as we shall see. The success of the Model F was truly staggering, with some three quarters of a million units being produced in eleven years!

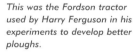

This was the Fordson tractor used by Harry Ferguson in his experiments to develop better ploughs.

THE FORD MOTOR COMPANY

Henry Ford built his first car in 1896, a quadricycle. His association with Alexander Y Malcomson, whose Coal Company supplied the Edison Company in Detroit where Ford was chief engineer, led to Malcomson's interest in Henry Ford's racing exploits. Ford's first two attempts at floating companies failed, but with the incorporation of the Ford Motor Company on 16th June 1903, it was third time lucky and the company was to grow into a world leader.

The first milestone on the road to success was the launch of the Model T in 1908. It was indeed with a conversion of this very car that Harry Ferguson began his work on mounted ploughs. The Model T was produced until 1927. Meanwhile in 1917 the Fordson tractor, whose history is described elsewhere, went into production.

The retooling for the Model A in 1927 lost Ford a lot of business but expansion was under way elsewhere in the world, including the building of Ford's English plant at Dagenham, east of London. The Ford V8 was introduced in 1932 and in 1939 the Mercury V8 model was launched. It was this car which provided many of the components, along with others from Ford's truck range, which enabled the Ford Ferguson 9N to go into production so quickly.

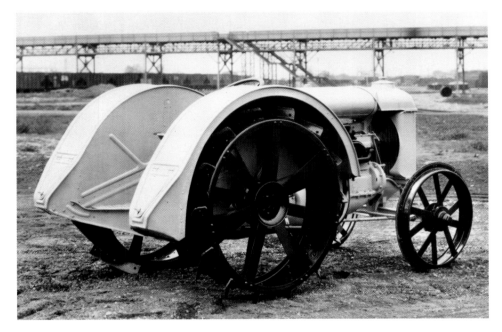

A late example of the Model F with fenders fitted. These are of the later pattern with built-in toolboxes.

An early Muir Hill dumper based on the Fordson F tractor.

IRISH INTERLUDE 1929-32

Above: A typical Cork built Model N tractor of the 1929-31 period.

Below: The narrow-winged example shown here typifies the late Cork period. The narrow wings did not last for long!

Although sales of the original Fordson tractor in Britain, by the standards set in later years, were relatively modest, the lack of a cheap, mass-produced tractor for the British market was taken up by Percival Perry, head of the Ford Company in the United Kingdom, who suggested that such a tractor should be built in England. The new Ford plant at Dagenham in Essex was then being built and it was expected that it would be ready in 1932, but this left a period when there would be no tractors to sell. At this time spare capacity was available at the Ford plant at Cork in Ireland. It was therefore decided that production of the tractor should be undertaken there.

*Above: An early 1930s
demonstration of the hill
climbing prowess of a Ford
Model A truck, using a Cork
built Fordson N as the load.*

*Left: A Cork built Fordson N
converted for use in the
hopfields of Kent.*

15

By comparison with the massive production levels of the Model F at the Dearborn plant in the USA, which built over 747,000 units in just under 11 years, that is to say an average of 68,000 units per year, the production levels at Cork were mediocre, with just under 10,000 units built in 1929, 15,000 in 1930 and 3,500 in 1931. Only just over 3,000 units were assembled in 1932. These were enough to meet the depressed demand for Fordsons in the United Kingdom and still leave some for export.

The Irish Build

The decision to produce the tractor in Ireland did allow for some updating to take place. Some of the features of the Fordson Model F were outdated by this time, such as the low tension flywheel magneto, the lack of a water pump and the flimsy front wheels.

Development work on the tractor was actually started in the USA, as the facilities in England were inadequate. A number of prototypes were assembled, and these showed certain Model F features not carried into production such as the use of Holley 295 Vaporisers, rear outlet fuel tanks, a revised transmission with an extra

PTO plate and a handbrake operating on band-type rear wheel brakes, all applied to at least one prototype. Strange to say, although the last Fordson Model Fs received the latest style of fenders with tapered-in rear panels and improved footboards, the new Model N development tractors came out with the old-style ones.

The HT American Bosch magneto was driven from the timing train and provision was made for a governor to be fitted in front of the housing on the right-hand side which carried the base mounted magneto. The transmission was beefed up, with better bearings and an improved transmission brake, and the engine was given an extra eighth of an inch in the bore. The aircleaner, although still water filled, was given a new housing which retained the sector steering beneath.

Production tractors differed only in some details. The fuel tank now had a central outlet, the Kingston MD type vaporiser was adopted and the magneto bracket was tidied up and reinforced. A catch was provided to hold the clutch down for parking rather than provide the expensive alternative of band brakes and the later type of fenders were fitted as standard.

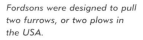

Fordsons were designed to pull two furrows, or two plows in the USA.

Cork was not the ideal place to build tractors as had been proved before with the ill-fated attempt at producing the Model F there from 1919 to 1921. Unfortunately, by the time the tractor was in production, the world trade depression was in full swing. As the production and sales figures for the Cork built tractors show, even though production was not at a high level, the prevailing economic conditions meant that sales of the tractors coming off the production line, were sluggish. Out of this adversity however, came opportunity. There was time to improve the tractor and make it ready for real mass production in the future which would be undertaken at Dagenham and not at Cork.

DAGENHAM DELIGHTS 1933-39

Fordson also produced an industrial model. One is seen here in the early 1930s, complete with a tipping refuse trailer.

Publicity artwork for the Dagenham built Fordson N standard agricultural model.

In 1932 the tractor went through a number of changes to make it more suitable for the UK market. Firstly, the cumbersome wings with their toolboxes went, in favour of ones with very narrow tops but of the same length. Then the whole driving position was redesigned. This set the driving position on agricultural Fordsons firmly to the rear for the rest of the tractor's production life. After a short sojourn in a pale blue finish with red wheels, a colour scheme applied to the last Cork built examples, the Essex farm cart colours of dark blue with orange wheels were adopted when the final Dagenham product arrived in 1933. Many components had now reached the stage where they would change very little in the next 12 years.

Pneumatic Tyres

The next important stage in the development of the tractor came in 1934 when
pneumatic tyres were offered factory fitted,
for the first time. In the next year, however,
proper land utility models were advertised,
complete with industrial type underslung
silencers, extra brakes as an option, bulb
horns and big side tool boxes with all the
equipment required to change and inflate
tyres. Industrial models had been available
from the outset in 1929. These retained the
upright steering and forward clutch pedal
of the 1929-32 model right through Model
N production. A handbrake operating band
brakes on the rear axle shafts and a 6-volt
lighting set were standard on this model.

On Three Wheels

Sales to the USA took an upturn in 1935/6
and the opportunity was taken to introduce
a rowcrop model aimed at this market. One
of the problems which had always beset the
Fordson before the Second World War was
the fact that, like its American predecessor,
the N never really made vast sums for the
Ford Motor Company. Any rowcrop version
had to be a cost-effective way of giving the
tractor an all-purpose appeal for that
transatlantic market.

Other manufacturers in the USA had produced similar, low-cost alternatives to a
standard model in rowcrop form and it is
no surprise that the looks of the Fordson
'All Around' as it was known in the USA (the
term rowcrop is preferred in the UK) bore
some resemblance to the Case CC rowcrop.
The front wheels were borne by a swan-
necked bracket attached to a redesigned
cylinder front cover, and at the rear end
independent brakes were fitted on the ends
of the rear axle housings. The rear wheel

*Tractors loaded in railway
wagons await shipment from
the Dagenham plant.*

19

track was extended by simply bolting splined extensions to the taper hubs on the normal half shafts, which on the standard tractor held the wheels in position. The track could be moved out to any desired position and fixed using the same taper bush on the rowcrop wheels as held the standard wheels in check. Wheels for the rowcrop were bought in from French & Hecht and the tractor was available in both steel wheeled and pneumatic tyred form with the alternative of steel or pneumatic vee twins on the front and skeleton steels or 9.00 x 36in pneumatics on the rear. The transmission was modified and a new gearbox introduced with a 4.3 mph top gear. This unit also allowed the fitment of a side PTO driven from the gearbox and henceforward all N transmissions were equipped with a plate on the right-hand side. The cylinder front cover was adopted for use with the straight front axle also, which had not been used since 1930. All tractors for export to the USA had straight axles from 1936 on. The reason for this was that a rowcrop conversion was marketed there, though it did not really take off and ceased to be advertised after a short time.

The Fordson rowcrop or 'All Around' was introduced for the American market. This is a 1938 example.

Top left: A close-up of an orange Fordson showing side toolbox and engine details.

Top right: Typical of 1941 tractors, this example once belonged to the author. As built it had steel rather than pneumatic wheels.

Left: The 1938 tractors were brightened up by painting them in a bright orange livery known as 'Harvest Gold'. This is a land utility example.

Bottom: 1939 saw economies; note the change to the mudguards. The colour was originally the same as the earlier tractors but the paint didn't wear well and this example has received a darker finish on restoration.

Outdated Features

Most Fordson models in 1936 still retained one rather outdated feature, the water air washer. This was a moot selling point in the USA where in certain winter conditions, the washer would freeze even with the tractor in service. The worm and sector steering fitted was also non adjustable.

The opportunity was taken to redesign the steering and fit a worm and pinion unit in its own housing, lubricated by extreme pressure oil. This was primarily done for the industrial tractor, but the Handy Governor Company of Detroit, owned by one William Ford, brother of Henry, was approached by Sherman & Sheppard to supply an alternative oil bath aircleaner which would fit the Model N. This they did, and some units were shipped to the UK for fitment to tractors as early as March 1936. The extra cost of the steering assembly and the aircleaner was a contributory factor to the units not being universally adopted sooner.

An Ailsa Craig diesel engine fitted into the Fordson.

A few tractors with Handy aircleaners were released into the UK market in 1936. The dealers asked for more but were told that as the components were imported, there was no chance of universal adoption. Export sales were foremost in the minds of those at Dagenham who controlled the purse strings and 1937 saw the first signs of the fashion for streamlining, which first emerged in the US market as competitors relaunched old favourites in attractive new tinwork and sprayed in bright colours.

Orange Is The Colour

Ford had to do something to keep up with this trend. A restyle of the Fordson was out of the question, but something had to be done to improve the tractor. What about better performance? There had been a gradual improvement in the quality of tractor fuels through the 1930s, due to technical advances in the fractional distillation of crude oil, with Tractor Vaporising Oils replacing regular Kerosine as the usual fuel.

The result was that an updated tractor was launched officially in the Autumn of 1937. This featured a raised compression ratio, new 9in wide rear wheels, a radiator blind, the Handy oilbath aircleaner and worm steering. It also sported a new 'harvest gold' colour scheme. Some blue-liveried tractors were built between July and October to the new specification. The intention had been to paint the wheels blue but in practice they remained orange.

The new model was reasonably well received in the USA where gasoline was the normal fuel, but on the ones sold in the UK, the pre-ignition from those uprated engines could be heard miles away! Not only that, when faced with hard work for any length of time they broke con-rods, crankshafts, big end and main bearings. Things had to be altered after a very short time to halt the flood of warranty claims. The technical problems were resolved eventually, but post-1937 Fordsons were always more temperature sensitive than the previous ones, and needed that radiator blind to keep them hot! The rowcrop was also given a new design of worm steering and better brakes in 1938.

Thoughts Of A New Model

The problems associated with the 1937/8 orange tractor did not help the finances.

PERKINS DIESELS

The diesel engine had been around for some time in various forms, indeed its application in heavy goods vehicles and public service vehicles had become almost universal by 1945. Various attempts had been made to launch diesel tractors onto the UK market, but most of these had fallen by the way-side. Strange to say there was not one totally new multi-cylin-dered diesel on the British tractor scene before the Second World War. A company called Agricultural and General Engineers offered tractors using Blackstone and Aveling engines which were basically International 22/36 frames with diesel engines fitted. A few International petrol-start diesels as fitted to their WD40 and TD35/40 crawlers were imported, but like the domestic conversions they did not amount to much. Mainstay of the compression ignition picture was the Marshall, but even here total production was small. As the majority of UK tractors were in any case multi cylinder units with automotive type engine and transmission layout, it was obvious that any manufacturer setting out to build tractor engines would adopt the multi-cylinder concept.

One of the immediate problems which arose in producing a diesel engine was its cost, not only in development terms, but in production also. Much finer tolerances were necessary and stronger components desirable to withstand the much greater compression pressures of such engines.

Barford & Perkins of Peterborough became part of Agricultural and General Engineers (AGE). Their main product line was motor road-rolling equipment. The Peterborough works was closed by AGE when they took over in 1928-29 and their road-roller business was merged with that of Aveling & Porter to form Aveling-Barford.

Frank Perkins moved to Aveling's works at Strood as works manager. It was while he was there that the Vixen engine was designed, the drawings being done by a. draughtsman employed by the aircraft manufacturer Short Brothers, work-ing at weekends in the cellar of Perkins' house. One or two engines were built at Aveling's before the big decision was made to set up a company to produce them.

Frank Perkins Ltd was formed and rented premises at Queen Street in Peterborough, formerly occupied by Barford & Perkins. This was a case of coming home; Frank Perkins obviously knew that the works were standing empty, and an approach to the owners, Milton Estates, secured a lease. Indeed, quite a lot of equipment, such as the work benches, was still there. Here in the 1930s the application of medium sized diesels for industrial and marine work was pioneered.

The Leopard, Wolf and Lynx engines were basically intended for multi-use applications, covering vehicle, indus-trial and marine installations. However, the use of the Leopard engine in tractors was instigated in the mid 1930s. A Fordson N land utility tractor on Firestone wheels and tyres

was supplied to F. Perkins Ltd on 11th February 1937 by the Willenhall, Staffordshire, Fordson dealer, Reginald Tildesley. This had the serial number 808499 and it was delivered to Peterborough without an engine.

A Perkins Leopard engine, serial number 7343, built on 16th June 1937, was fitted. This was a Leopard II engine with cast iron pistons and was rated at 34bhp at 1100 rpm, it being derated from the usual industrial rating of 46bhp at 1500rpm to prevent damage to the rear axle.

The prototype tractor was tried out at Tettenhall near Wolverhampton in July 1937, prior to its exhibition at the Royal Show, which in 1937 was held at the nearby Wrottesley Park.

In October and November 1937 a further 11 engineless tractors were supplied to Perkins by Tildesley, and in 1938/9 a further 17 were supplied, making 29 in all. Incidentally, the TVO engines from these tractors were used to provide a float for Tildesley's exchange engine scheme on Fordson tractors.

The first Leopard conversion to go into full-time farm ser-vice was bought by Mr T.R.C. Blofeld of Hoverton Fruit Farms, Wroxham, Norfolk. It had the reputation of being a bad starter, but the early models had no self starter and were started on the handle using a decompressor. It would appear that most of the others were exported, and there is at least one extant in Australia and another one in New Zealand. The latter example has a self starter. Another engine was also installed in a Muir Hill 3 cubic yard twin wheel dumper which appeared at the Public Works Exhibition at Olympia in London, in 1938. This also had an electric starter.

With the advent of the war, the conversion of tractors ceased, but in the meantime the development of a new range of engines was under way at Peterborough. These are dis-cussed in Chapter Five.

23

The sales boys were always applying pressure for an improved model and this gave the development team a chance to play around with new ideas, at least on the drawing board. They worked towards a new model with the engine uprated and given shell bearings, or possibly even an overhead valve layout. The other desire was for a tractor which did not have that worm and wheel transmission.

The main weakness of the Fordson was that the worm drive transmission had a greater power loss than other types. An Allis U rear end was fitted with a Fordson engine to see what results would be obtained with a bevel gear final drive. This proved promising and several other prototypes were built using different types of transmission. Some used transmissions produced by other manufacturers, others were developed from scratch. Experimental engines were produced too, including overhead valve and diesel units, but the coming of war in 1939 put an end to these experiments. Another factor in any case was that of cost. They had little chance of becoming reality due to the development costs involved being almost impossible to recover. Price was always a critical factor in Fordson sales, and immediate prewar estimates indicated that the basic model would cost £205 with only some of the modifications thought about! A steady increase in UK sales prior to 1938 was virtually halved in that year. In 1937 18,698 units were sold, this dropped to 10,647 in 1938. There was some recovery in 1939 when 15,712 units were sold as some panic buying may have taken place as war clouds loomed.

Fortunes Of War

As it happened, the events leading up to the 3rd September 1939 had not gone unnoticed by the powers that be, and as soon as war broke out, all materials came under the control of the Ministry of Supply, and everything made, from a pin to a battleship, had to have government approval. Three agencies affected Fordson tractor production. The first was the Ministry of Supply, which controlled the distribution of all materials required to build any further machines once existing stocks had been used up. They were also a customer for Fordson tractors as these were used by the armed forces and government departments. The second agency was the National Federation of Vehicle Trades, an organisation set up by both the Ministry of Supply and the Ministry of War Transport. The third interested party was not surprisingly, the Ministry of Agriculture. The latter appointed County War Agricultural Executives to monitor the need for increased mechanisation on farms in the face of the necessity to greatly increase the country's production of food in response to the threat of blockades and attacks on shipping by the German navy.

In the case of the Fordson, its basic specification could not be pruned that much, and it was deemed a national necessity to maintain continuity of production. The supply of parts for tractor production was not frozen whereas other areas of the motor industry such as the production of bus chassis, were severely curtailed or prohibited. The free allocation of units to dealers was halted early in 1940. After this a permit from the Local War Agricultural Executive had to be obtained in order to purchase a new tractor.

The Fordson specification as it existed in September 1939 was left unchanged. The only real differences between the 1939 model and the 1938 one involved the availability of 28in rear wheels on the land utility model, and further messing about with the engine and some of its components. There were supply problems with some components, notably the German Bosch FU4B magneto. After a period when American made Bosch magnetos were used, Lucas came up with their GJ4 unit which was fitted to all but a few Fordsons thereafter.

Above: The Land Army was a British government organisation which employed mainly women to increase the country's agricultural output. Here some Land Army girls are seen shifting timber with the help of a 1940 Fordson.

Left: Steel wheeled tractors needed road bands to move them along the public highway. This 1944 solution was to fit tyres to the outside of the normal rear wheels.

A 1938 Fordson industrial as supplied to the RAF.

This 1939 land utility tractor was also impressed into war work for the Royal Air Force. It is seen here in front of a Halifax bomber.

Savings Made

Some economies were made as production was stepped up to meet the demands laid down by the government agencies. The first was the cropping of mudguard front plates; this not only saved metal but assembly time. Then, as more and more Land Army girls took the wheel, feedback through the WACs indicated that several minor items might be improved to ease the lot of the fair sex when

dealing with the temperamental old Fordson. The steering drag link was replaced by a spring-loaded affair and a shorter drop arm was fitted to ease steering effort. A hole appeared in the radiator side to facilitate access to the sparking plugs and instruction plates on the tanks were provided to tell the amateur how to start the thing! Finally, calormeters appeared on radiator tops to prevent the girls being burned on performing the time honoured technique of feeling the radiator bottom tank to see if it was hot!

Between 1936 and 1939, the popularity of fitting pneumatic tyres to agricultural tractors increased. A large number of these were also fitted with extra braking equipment. The restraints placed on the availability of rubber meant that by 1941 virtually all Fordson production of the standard agricultural model had reverted to steel wheels. Only a limited number of pneumatic tyred land utility tractors were produced, and these were either sent to the forces for use on airfields or in stores areas, or were available on special allocation through the County War Agricultural Committees, to farmers who had a need to use a tractor on the road. The WACs also used these units themselves to transport fuel, implements and other tractors.

Further changes to the wartime tractors were minor. Mudguard to dash brackets were made from pressed steel from late 1941 onwards and in 1942 a further saving of materials was accomplished by reducing the mudguard tops to a mere rolled strip some 5in wide. Manifold shields became the norm as did those blessed 'torpedoes' in fuel and air passages. Then in 1944 a new-style vaporiser mixing chamber came along with a diaphragm-type economy device attached. Land utility tractors with brakes still featured the wide wings until stocks were used up. Indeed some tractors built as late as November 1944 are known to have had wide wings.

One important change did take place from November 1940, the adoption of an all over green paint finish. This was done to prevent the tractors being easily seen from the air, especially when parked on the wharf at Dagenham. The Luftwaffe used the River Thames as a corridor to guide aircraft in to bomb central London, and so any landmarks such as a mass of orange on the riverside needed to be eliminated.

Finale

Production had been running at over 100 units a day at its peak during the Second World War. Of the tractors produced only a small percentage were anything other than standard agricultural units. Rowcrops continued to be built in small batches, indeed the delays in getting the E27N out meant that a final batch of rowcrops had to be built in 1945 after Ford had officially said that there would be no more. Industrial models were also built. This model had changed least since the Cork days. It retained the short steering column and forward driving position, but was fitted with a handbrake, 6-volt lighting set and the standard wheel equipment was in the form of high pressure

pneumatic tyres. Originally, solid rubber tyred wheels had been available. The War Department preferred low pressure tyres for their needs, and indeed some industrials so equipped were supplied in 1938 for RAF use. The wartime contract S8226 specified low pressure tyres and these tractors had 28in rears. In addition to complete tractors, around 13,000 Fordson Ns were supplied in 'skid unit' form to various concerns for conversion into a multiplicity of equipment. Though production of the replacement model, the E27N, should have started in January 1945, the usual delays meant that in fact, the last Model N was not built until 4th June of that year.

Afterlife

The Fordson N story did not end in 1945 however. There were still restrictions on the sale of new tractors until 1949/50, and the wartime role of the Fordson as used by the government agencies during the conflict brought mechanisation to many farms which had previously only used horses. Great sales of surplus equipment took place in the early postwar years as the tractors owned and run by the County War Agricultural Committees were sold. There were also a substantial number of ex-RAF, army and navy Fordsons disposed of at the same time.

The abundance of secondhand units in the marketplace might have worried Ford, but they knew that as long as these tractors were in use they could sell parts and service. Because the new E27N used so many N components, there was a continued availability of spares. Not only this, some components which had been improved for use on the E27N found their way onto Model Ns. These included magnetos, glass bowl fuel filters, improved governors and exhausts. Later, many Ns were fitted with the 1950 vaporiser conversion for which special assemblies were available to suit the standard tractor.

Many of the Fordsons which survived into the 1950s and 60s were therefore not as they were built. The Ford reconditioned engine scheme was soon extended to the Fordson. Whilst early replacement engines had N-style blocks without the starter aperture, rationalisation soon took place with the E27N block being used for all reconditioned units with only the crankshaft being different.

The Bits Business

There was also a vast business in replacement parts from other sources; what we in the Ford dealer network used to call, non Ford parts. A look at a Kerry's catalogue from the late 1940s shows the many non Ford parts that were on the market for use on Fordsons. The favourite non standard unit on the Fordson was the vaporiser. The temperamental hotplate equipment with

which the Fordson was endowed gave an ideal excuse for many and varied local engineers to create alternatives marketed under such names as the BEC, Loddon, Fishleigh, Elliot & Hadden and many others, which endeavoured to try and improve on the Fordson vaporiser's performance. In fact the old-type vaporiser when set up properly is, in the opinion of your author, by far the best in terms of power output and general performance.

The other postwar business which gave dealers a boom time was the supply of pneumatic tyres and wheels once restrictions on their availability were lifted. The vast majority of 1941-45 Fordsons still in existence today started life on steel wheels and received pneumatic tyre conversions in the late 1940s and early 1950s. Again the proprietory suppliers got in on the act with wheel centres and there are as many varia-

The 150,000th Fordson built at Dagenham comes off the line on the 29th March 1943. The tractor is typical of the wartime design from 1942 with the economy fenders. Every day, 100 of these units rolled off the production line.

tions in these as would fill a whole book on that subject alone. Add to this the variety of drawbar attachments and other gadgets and it is no wonder that, though in theory all Fordsons should be the same, yet in practice they are nearly all different. Some of the most remarkable transformations befell ex-RAF tractors which in the main were built with low pressure tyres. When these were converted for agricultural use, they acquired vaporisers, governors, mudguards and standard drawbars and some were even fitted with new steering columns and oilbath aircleaners to turn them into standard Fordsons.

A wartime Fordson N restored and used in vintage ploughing competitions. The red wheels are not original, all-over green being the order of the day when the tractor was new.

Diesel Conversions - Certainly Not!

One area in which Ford did stand its ground was in the matter of diesel conversion packs for the N. The Ford board felt that for F Perkins Limited to offer a conversion pack for the N would be to artificially prolong the life of what was becoming an obsolete tractor. They had written into agreements for the supply of Ford parts for the conversion packs, and the purchase of P series engines for Ford factory fitting that, 'the fitting of the Perkins P6(TA) engine into the old-style Fordson tractor is not recommended'. Some conversions were done, a very few, to suit individual customers, and there has in recent times been an upsurge in fitting Fordson Ns with P6(TA) and L4 engines for use in vintage ploughing matches, something which was never intended for them.

Demise

The faithful Fordsons soldiered on. Often they were to be found on smaller farms into the fifties and even the early sixties. As secondhand Fergie 20s started to flood the market when the diesel tractor really got a grip in the mid fifties, the faithful 'Henries' were relegated to standby and harvest work. They were prized targets of the diddicoys as they collected scrap around the countryside. These gentlemen used to offer

a farmer around £10 for the tractor in the early sixties knowing full well that the phosphor bronze worm wheel alone was worth double that. Your author can well remember finding tractors in hedge bottoms in the late sixties which had been sold to the 'diddys' and as they could not be towed, the radiator core would be smashed out at one end and the sledgehammer or gas axe used to open up the rear axle and extract the worm wheel at the other. There was a catch however, as some wartime builds had a steel worm wheel. I have even come across one of these where the tractor had been smashed to get it out, and on finding that the worm wheel was a steel one, it was just left beside the debris! The smarter scrapmen always offered less money for a utility model, one with narrow wings.

Fortunately the Fordson N has fared well in the hands of preservationists, with what must be many hundreds of these tractors now restored and taken to rallies and ploughing matches, not only in the United Kingdom, but throughout the world in territories where the tractors were originally sold.

Chapter Four

TRACTORS FOR HARRY FERGUSON - 1939-1952

The prototype Ford Ferguson 9N.

The end of tractor production in the United States in 1928 was a source of regret for Henry Ford, so when the opportunity to resume tractor building came about through an agreement with the Harry Ferguson, Henry Ford seized it. He had first met Ferguson in 1920 when the latter was demonstrating his plough at Dearborn. Now nearly 20 years later, Ferguson was demonstrating his Model A tractor and plough at Henry Ford's residence at Fair Lane. The two men quickly came to an agreement for Ford to build a tractor in the USA equipped with the Ferguson hydraulic system. The famous 'Handshake Agreement' provided for Ford to build the tractors and Ferguson to market them through his own selling organisation.

With the benefit of the most up-to-date developments in automotive engineering, the Ford design team, along with Ferguson's men Sands and Greer, created the real forerunner of the modern tractor. To speed production the use of standard components was encouraged, and apart from the Ferguson Hydraulic System, the tractor showed its Ford parentage very well in the use of an engine which was half a Mercury V8, and a transmission and other components common with other contemporary Ford products. The rear axle design was based on Ford's light truck range and this was to prove a weakness when extra power was required in later years.

Speedy Development

Prototypes were to hand in March 1939, and by June production models were available for demonstration. The tractor was very much in line with contemporary Ford styling, and the four-cylinder side valve engine of 3.125in bore by 3.75in stroke developed 24hp at a maximum speed of 2,200rpm. The engine was machined on the same line as the V8 units, an additional shift being put on to cope with the extra production.

Just how much Ferguson's team influenced the design is subject to question, as Ford design policy was very much the work of a team effort rather than being dominated by individuals. Ferguson's men just became, pro tem, part of that team. Certainly the hydraulic linkage was pure Ferguson, but the incorporation of the hydraulic pump into a square transmission housing seems to have originated with Charles Sorensen. The beam-type front axle was the work of Sands and Greer. Ferguson himself would have liked to have seen an overhead valve engine fitted to the tractor, but the costs of development and timescale for planned production ruled this out.

The selling organisation which was set up also included the Sherman brothers, who had sold Ferguson ploughs earlier on. The new sales organisation was in part financed by a loan of $50,000 from Henry Ford. The tractor, the 9N, was an instant success and put behind it all the weaknesses of the type A.

England - A No-Go Area.

There was, however, nothing in the agreement in the USA to allow for production of the Ford 9N in the United Kingdom. Ford of Britain were virtually independent of the parent US concern in 1939. Attempts were made to get 9N production started in the UK, but Percival Perry, head of Ford in Britain, found himself drawn into some rather unfortunate politics concerning Henry Ford.

Ford, who was recovering from the after-effects of a stroke, was not in full command of the situation, and the attempts by him to force Dagenham to produce the 9N caused a rift between Perry and himself. In any case the matter was now in fact outside Perry's hands, as the war in Europe had effectively placed tractor production under government control and there was no way the government would allow a break in production to happen.

The 9N did reach the United Kingdom, fitted with a modified Holley 295 Vaporiser

The engine of the Ford Ferguson 9N was effectively half a Mercury V8 unit.

to run on TVO and designated the 9NAN. Ford in the United Kingdom handled all spares and service on these units which were imported under wartime lend-lease arrangements.

Wartime shortages led to a utility model being produced in the United States. This had steel wheels, and did not have battery-reliant electrics or a self starter. The 2NAN was the British equivalent of this model.

Edsel Ford, Henry Ford's oldest son, who had a hand in styling the 9N, died in 1943. This left a gap in the Ford empire filled by Henry Ford II, grandson of the founder, in 1945. The new chairman had the onerous task of putting the Ford operation back into the black after the ravages of war, and his attitude to the production of a tractor sold by another organisation was hostile. Henry Ford II realised that the bad business judgement of his father had created a serious problem. Had there been a simple agreement in writing rather than the ambiguity of the Handshake Agreement, many of the later unpleasantries might have been avoided when Ford terminated the sales agreement in 1947.

Above: The Ford Ferguson 9N inherited much of its styling from contemporary Ford trucks.

Right: After the end of the Handshake Agreement the Ford 8N offered most of the features found on the 9N.

HARRY FERGUSON

Harry Ferguson was born at Growell, County Down , in what is now Northern Ireland, on the 4th November 1884. He was a son of a farmer, one of 11 children. He did not care much for farm work but soon found that he had a natural aptitude for mechanical work. Ferguson, like so many of his fellow countrymen, considered emigrating to the United States of America. Instead he joined his elder brother Joe in his car and motorcycle business in Belfast in 1902

Harry was an aviation pioneer and had built and flown his own machine by 1909. After building several more aircraft, the demands of married life caused him to give up this dangerous pastime for a less hazardous one, that of racing cars and motor cycles. In 1911 he established May Street Motors in Belfast and sold the Waterloo Boy tractor in Ireland. This machine was sold in Britain as the Overtime.

His preoccupation with tractors and agricultural machinery was to take up more and more of his time. His first designs were for ploughs. By the 1920s, he was taking out patents on elements of what later became the Ferguson System. In attempting to further his cause of bringing the Ferguson System to the world, he not only wooed but was wooed by most of the major tractor manufacturers at some time or other.

A key element in the Ferguson story was the involvement of others. David Brown, the Ford Motor Company and the Standard Motor Company all played an important part in the development of the tractors to which the Ferguson System was applied. Ferguson himself had built up his own design team, the key members of which were Willie Sands and Archie Greer.

Ferguson moved as the need arose, taking property in Yorkshire during the David Brown years at Honley, near Meltham. His English home became Abbotswood, an estate near Stow on the Wold in Gloucestershire. His English headquarters were at Fletchampstead Highway in Coventry, not far from the Banner Lane plant of Standard Motor Company where his tractors were built. After his company merged with Massey Harris, Harry Ferguson held the chair of Massey-Harris-Ferguson Ltd. However, he resigned once it became clear that his LTX prototypes for a bigger tractor would not reach production.

His activities then centred on other interests including the development of four-wheel-drive vehicles and the design and construction of racing cars. Harry Ferguson Research had been formed in 1950 and this organisation continued after his death in 1960. One ironic note is that HF Research was involved in the development of the BMC mini tractor. What if Morris Motors had taken up the challenge in the beginning?

But what sort of man was this son of Ulster soil? Like many great inventors his behaviour at times was somewhat eccen-

tric. He had fixed ideas about many things, for example he insisted that all involved in his business wore single-35 suits, expressly when demonstrating equipment. He also demanded punctuality at all times and if people turned up late for an appointment, he sometimes would refuse to see them. He suffered from bouts of depression when things were not going well and whilst giving much inspiration to those he partnered in his business activities, most of these relationships failed with the other parties involved with Ferguson driven to exasperation.

Despite these failings, the world has to thank Harry Ferguson for something with which nearly every tractor in use in this new century is equipped, the three point linkage and draft control. His work led the revolution which has eventually brought the benefits of mechanisation to agriculture and food production across the globe.

The Break

The relationship between Ferguson and Ford had sadly deteriorated, not helped by wartime shortages and the end result was that by 1948 Ford were building their own tractor, the 8N, which was simply an improved 9N, and selling it through their own sales organisation. The new Ford tractor had a four-speed rather than a three-speed gearbox and improved hydraulics with a means of overriding the Ferguson draft control. By this time of course the TE-20, a tractor of very similar design to the 8N, was being built in England.

The end of the agreement left Ferguson with no tractors to sell in America. He was forced to import such tractors as he could from England. He therefore filed a complaint against the Ford Motor Company on 8th January 1948, relating to patents held by him and used on the hydraulic system on the Ford tractor.

The trial started on 29th March 1951. The sum of $240,000,000 was claimed as a result of the introduction of the Ford 8N and the consequent loss in business to the Ferguson organisation, and the unlicenced use of the Ferguson system, which was patented, on the new Ford tractor. After long and costly proceedings, Ferguson accepted a settlement of $9,250,000. This was only to cover the unauthorised use of the Ferguson hydraulic system, the claim against loss of business was dismissed.

The Ford Motor Company were instructed to stop production of the Dearborn or 8N tractor by 1952, but the Ferguson patents had already been extended and were soon to be out of date. Ford's new 1951 model, the NAA, had a fully live hydraulic system with an engine-driven hydraulic pump and its introduction necessitated the updating of the then current TO-20 model in due course. Most modern

The Ford Ferguson 9N used the latest automobile technology with coil ignition and electric starting.

Above: During the war certain economies were introduced and the model 2N was launched. This restored 2N has been upgraded with lights and a self starter.

Left: The Ford 8N was the tractor that brought about the famous lawsuit between Ferguson and Ford.

tractors now have the draft control pioneered by Harry Ferguson, usually with the Ford innovation of the 36 feature which allows the lift to be used under position control. This latter feature was not approved by Ferguson, yet from the 35 on it became standard on all Massey-Ferguson models. In due course manufacturers such as Ford and M-F often came to reciprocal agreements over the use of each other's patents. So complex had the situation become over these that M-F and other makers set up their own patents departments run by lawyers to ensure that any new ideas they had were covered, and also to make sure that in building anything new they were not in infringement of anybody else's patented designs.

A MAJOR MANIFESTATION 1945-1952

By virtue of being the largest manufacturer of tractors in the United Kingdom, the Ford Motor Company was able to maintain a high level of production of its Model N throughout the Second World War. The production line on which this model was produced was well nigh worn out by 1945, but it was not possible to retool and re-equip the plant to launch a completely new model. Firstly, the sophisticated machine tools required to cope with a new engine for such a tractor were not available from UK manufacturers, and spending precious dollars was discouraged by the post war British government. The continued need for tractors meant that the model could not be altered too much if production was to be maintained.

The Festival of Britain featured a specially prepared Fordson Major E27N on a hydraulic ram. The wheels rotated electrically.

A typical mid-period land utility Fordson Major.

Right: After sale, no two E27Ns remained the same for long. This 1951 built example has the later vaporiser and non-standard back wheels.

Below: Electric lighting and starting were optional and examples with and without these features can be seen here.

Above: This 1950 Rowcrop model is equipped with a Howard 2:1 reduction gearbox sandwiched between the normal gearbox and rear axle.

Right: The three point linkage and hydraulic lift fitted to the E27N was a straight up and down affair but the configuration does enable modern implements to be attached as seen here.

Wartime Needs

Consultation with the War Agricultural Committees identified the need for a tractor which could plough three furrows instead of two, have a rowcrop capability with higher ground clearance than the N, and have a central PTO. In addition, the capability of the tractor taking a three point linkage and being self starting, were added by Ford, although these features did not appear until later. To get the ground clearance and greater power, the old worm and wheel transmission of the Fordson was replaced by a new double reduction rear axle with spiral bevel drive on the bull pinion shaft, a feature copied from various US designs, such as the Massey Harris 203 and the International Farmall. The result was the E27N (E = English, 27 = 27HP, N = tractor). Some 60% of the parts used in ini-

Top: Chaseside Engineering used the E27N as a base for their rope operated shovels. A P6-engined example is seen here.

Above left: A Chaseside one ton crane handles casting components.

Above right: A Bray hydraulic loading shovel based on the E27N.

39

TVO and diesel engined
examples of the E27N expertly
restored by the Symingtons
from Fife, Scotland.

tial production were the same as used by
the previous model, a further 10% were
modified N parts, and the final 30% were
new, mainly in the area of the rear axle.

Unlike its predecessor which was sold in
industrial and pneumatic tyred (land utility) forms, it was available in two forms initially: standard agricultural, which had
fixed track, steel wheels, and no independent brakes; and the rowcrop, which had a
beam type front axle adjustable for width,
independent brakes and steel wheels, the
rear wheels being adjustable for width by
juxtaposition of the hub and rim. The land
utility, which had fixed track, brakes, and
pneumatic tyres, did not arrive until mid
1945, nor did the rowcrop with a pneumatic tyre option.

Alterations were required to the assembly line for the new model. The major problem which arose was that the new units

would not go through the old paint plant
without causing problems, so the all over
green finish applied by a series of fixed jets
mounted on hoops around the track gave
way to hand held guns, and a new colour
scheme, a return to the old blue and orange
of the pre-1938 models. In fact the first
E27Ns were taken off the line before painting and finished at the end of the truck line.

There was very little evidence of extras
on the first 12 months production. Indeed
the facility for self starting was there on the
block, but it took until March 1946 before
ring gears were fitted to the flywheel. At the
same time, the rather flimsy drawbar gave
way to a more substantial affair. As is always
the case, a number of modifications were
evident after the initial production tractors
went into service and weaknesses were
found. As patterns wore out further alterations were made to the design with the

effect that this removed more and more of the pure N features.

There is always an advantage in building a model which is a derivative of a previous one, and this manifests itself in the availability of spare parts for both the old tractor and the new. With many parts common to both the N and the E27N models, this made for continuity in the supply of spares. This also ensured that parts for the model the new tractor replaced, were guaranteed. Indeed, certain what one might term exclusively E27N components found their way onto earlier models whether recommended for service or not. Magnetos, fuel taps, steering components and improved governors and manifolds all found their way onto the N in service.

The first Fordson Major E27N fitted with a Perkins P6 engine by Frank Perkins for his own use.

The development tractor fitted with a Perkins L4(TA) engine for the Ford Motor Company.

THE PERKINS P SERIES

The Perkins P series engines came onto the market in the early war years. The basic design was planned from the outset to be capable of modification to produce three, four and six cylinder units. These had many common parts

The Perkins P6(TA) engine fitted neatly into the Fordson Major E27N. This is the prototype installation.

A much later production example of the P6(TA) fitted to the E27N.

and this saved much in development and production costs. Incidentally, one and two cylinder prototypes were built but were never produced in any quantity, and it took some time before the three cylinder variant, the P3, appeared. In fact, one P3 prototype was built in 1939, and fitted in a London taxi, but it was to be 1951-52 before this engine was fully developed. The P series originally had names as had the other pre-war engines. The P6 was the

Panther, the P4 the Puma and the P3 the Python. In fact, the P4 was introduced in November 1937 and the P6 in February 1938. There were of course two versions of the P series. That for use in applications where engine speeds of over 1,500rpm were required had aluminium alloy pistons, and that for use where engine speeds of below 1,500rpm were required had cast iron pistons. The calibration of the fuel injection pump produced engines with very different torque characteristics. All the three, four and six cylinder variants shared the same bore and stroke of 3.5in x 5in. The swept volumes were P3 - 2.36 litres; P4 - 3.14 litres and P6 - 4.73 litres.

The design of the engines was such that different sumps, flywheel housings, front and side mounting plates, and exhaust/inlet manifolds allowed a diversity of use, whether with a wet clutch application used on the Fordson Major, or a dry one such as on the Massey Harris 744D. For vehicle use of course, the mountings were different, but the sump used with industrial applications had sufficient strength, when necessary, to include the engines in unit applications.

There was even a petrol version of the P6, developed in conjunction with Dennis Brothers of Guildford, to replace their equivalent petrol engine, though only two of these experimental petrol engines were built.

The first P series engine to be fitted to tractor was used in a Ford Ferguson 9N, fitted with an early P4 unit. The next tractor to be adapted was the Fordson Major and in due course Perkins offered conversion packs for many make and models of tractors.

The P3, P4 and P6 were all offered in what was called TA or tractor adapted form to convert a number of spark ignition models to diesel, among them the Ford Ferguson 9N and the old Fordson Major E27N.

After Sales Service

There was always one big disadvantage with the E27N, and that was the engine. It was outdated technologically and this made overhaul a somewhat cumbersome operation. Unlike current automotive practice, blocks were cast with cylinders in place and the connecting rods and main bearings were direct metalled. Quite sophisticated equipment had been developed at the dealers for the overhaul and machining of blocks, and oversize pistons were available, but on the whole the sheer physical number of tractors in service by 1947 meant that dealers could not cope with overhauls, and thus a new scheme had to be instituted.

Thus it was that in 1949, the tractor reconditioned engine scheme was launched at the Smithfield show in December of that year. Initially a float of new blocks were launched of both N and E27N types and serviceable engines, less manifold, magneto bracket, cylinder front cover and plugs were returned to the factory for overhaul. Crankshafts were reground and blocks remettled, dry liners were fitted to the bores and all blocks were brought back to standard. Engines of this type were identified by the tag on a cylinder head bolt which advised which type of crankshaft was fitted. In fact the supply of N blocks eventually dried up and it became necessary to use E27N blocks with N crankshafts and flywheels, hence the need for identification. The original engine number was ground off and a new number was stamped on the left-hand clutch flange. The dealer was supposed to stamp the original engine and chassis numbers on the new engine but many didn't bother, hence the problem in dating tractors nowadays. In retrospect it is a pity that the proposed development of the same engine to incorporate more modern features such as shell bearings did not take place, as it would have helped gain an edge on the competition!

The second development tractor fitted with a Perkins P6(TA) engine for Ford. It was this engine which was chosen for production examples.

Perkins power became a very popular way to upgrade Fordson tractors and the two photographs above demonstrate various examples found on Cambridgeshire farms.

Left: An E27N using TVO working with a pickup baler.

P6 engined E27Ns are much sought after by preservationists. The splendid example from the Symington stable is seen above, whilst another tractor, this time fitted with a cab, is seen below.

A Diesel Engined E27N

It is all very well prolonging the life of tractors with an obsolete engine, but when the need arises to provide a diesel variant, it may sound strange that the engine manufacturer had more to do with this than the tractor builder. The Perkins P series had not been used widely in tractors until Frank Perkins converted a Fordson Major for his own use. The result was that the Ford Motor Company sent two Majors for conversion, one with a P4, and the other a P6 engine. Both had fabricated sumps and flywheel housings. Whilst both gave a satisfactory performance, the P6 was chosen due to its lower maximum speed which suited the E27N gearbox better. In adopting the engine as a production option it also must be remembered that the Ford dealer network was already geared up for Perkins spares and service as the engine in its vehicle (V) form was fitted in the Ford Thames lorry. So it came to pass that the P6(TA) engine was born and graced 23,259 E27Ns either off the production line or through the conversion packs which Perkins sold itself.

A total of 233,112 Fordson Majors were built between 1945 and 1952. A high proportion were exported, making 209,853 units fitted with the Fordson s.i. engine. Headaches occurred for Ford especially in the form of competition from the 'Grey Menace', the Ferguson 20, and there were also other manufacturers on the scene by 1950, who although not capable of building as many tractors as Ford, if they had a good dealer and salesmen in a certain area, could knock holes in home sales.

Although Ford knew what sort of tractor it would have liked to build in 1945, it was not able to give the machine its proper engine. In some ways the E27N was a stopgap. That its basic transmission and rear axle survived until 1964 in the E1A range said something for the original design, weak though it was at first.

It is easy to date components on surviving E27Ns. All major castings have a letter/figure/letter code set into the pattern at the time of casting which enables the exact date of casting to be ascertained.

Photograph on opposite page: On the binder with a Fordson Major E27N converted to diesel using the Perkins L4(TA) engine.

Left: An E27N powered by the Perkins L4(TA) engine. This engine, launched in 1953, was never fitted in production models.

Above: A beet harvesting demonstration with a Fordson Major E27N pitted against a Massey Harris 744D. The tractors are working in tandem with the harvester Fordson powered and the trailer hauled by the Massey Harris machine.

Below: A brand new P6(TA) powered E27N rowcrop is unloaded at a dealer's premises.

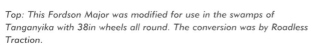

Top: This Fordson Major was modified for use in the swamps of
Tanganyika with 38in wheels all round. The conversion was by Roadless
Traction.

Above: An offside view of the Fordson Major E27N showing engine
details.

Above right: An Australian E27N with P6(TA) engine. The spark
arrestor and distinctive wheels were fitted in Australia as tractors were
shipped without wheels.

Right: A late TVO powered E27N in preservation.

DIESELS FOR ALL 1952-1964

The New Fordson Major in agricultural and industrial forms.

We have seen that the E27N Major was something of a stop-gap and when the time came to get rid of the obsolete features of that model, we need to understand that engine development is an expensive business. We also have to look at what other engines Ford were producing in the late 1940s to see the way ahead.

The Spark ignition engine as fitted to the New Fordson Major E1ADKN.

Besides the trusty old 4380cc side valve tractor unit inherited from the Model N there were also the eight and ten horsepower small bore units, which found application in some tractors, though not ones built by Ford, and the V8 which was not only used in the car of that name, but as a power unit in the Thames series of trucks. If a diesel was required, the Perkins P6V was the unit for the lorries, and the P6(TA) was used for the tractors.

Savings Made

A new tractor required a new engine. The type developed by Ford became known as the E1A. To cut development costs, it had to be capable of being used in all types of vehicles. It also had to be be able to be converted to use any type of fuel, diesel, petrol, even a vaporising oil, and could be built in four and later six cylinder forms. The type of fuel pump dictated the performance characteristics of the diesel and the carburettor the performance of the petrol version. The six cylinder units did not appear until 1957, and were not initially designed for tractors, but as we will see later they did find some use.

The great advance in engine design which the Ford development team achieved was a considerable measure of common parts between the spark ignition and compression ignition engines. This again reduced production costs, and helped the parts suppliers in that it reduced the number of spares that had to be kept in stock. As it happened, with something new, the modifications in the first five years of production were to prove somewhat of a parts and service manager's nightmare, but for the first time a diesel engine which actually started well and came out at a reasonable cost, was to grace many applications.

Not only did Ford fit the engines to their own Thames range of trucks and tractors, but sales of the units for industrial and other uses made the E1A engine one of the best sellers of the fifties and early sixties. Just like the old Fordson tractor and the numerous conversions thereof, there were few uses to which the new range of engines were not put.

The New Fordson Major with County full tracks.

Something Old, Something New

This tractor was very much based on the E27N. As far as transmission layout was concerned, even the front axle was identical, but skillful redesign of the gearbox (based on the 7.7 High Top Green Spot unit) added a primary box in front and thus gave the tractor six forward and two reverse gears. The hydraulics were different, the top PTO was abandoned, and the hydraulic pump installed in the rear transmission driven from the normal PTO and taking its oil supply from the rear axle's nine gallon capacity. Linkage was very similar to the old E27N, there being no depth control at this stage.

It was in the engines that Ford broke new ground. As already described, three versions were available in the tractor on its launch in November 1951, diesel, TVO, and petrol. The diesel and TVO used the same 100mm bore whilst the petrol was 97mm. It goes without saying that the diesel was an instant success and with the TVO engine being somewhat of a fuel guzzler and awkward to start to boot, it was the New Fordson Major that firmly established the high-speed diesel engine as a prime mover on our farms. From 1952 on the trend was away from low-cost fuel engines with the inconvenience of the need to carry a separate supply of petrol to start the engine. If there was a tractor which spelt the death knell of the TVO engine, it was the New Fordson Major.

The engine with its multiple applications was not self stressed and had to be supported by a sub-frame in the form of two channels bolted to the sides of the clutch housing, and with its own cast front to take either the usual front axle or a vee twin unit made by Roadless for export. Styling was attractive, possibly the best of the postwar designs, with a fuel tank to the rear of the engine and a hinged bonnet between this and the radiator cowl.

A new line was set up to build the New Fordson Major within the Dagenham complex and production soon settled down to a satisfactory level with an eventual proclamation from the sales department that the tractor was exported to 100 territories!

In the first analysis, the performance of the New Major was not outstanding. The power output represented a modest increase on the previous TVO model and a considerable decrease on the Perkins diesel engined unit. The first published figures for this tractor are as follows:

Belt Horsepower	Diesel	Petrol	TVO
Engine Speed 1,400rpm	34	33	32
Engine Speed 1,600rpm	37	35	34

Drawbar Horsepower	Diesel	Petrol	TVO
Max db hp	29.75	29.0	28.2
Speed mph	3.40	3.42	3.44

As can be seen, these figures were nothing special, indeed with the E27N capable of producing 26.6 for a VO tractor, and the P6 engined E27N recording 34/41 HP on test (that is 34 at the drawbar in 2nd gear, and 41 at the belt), these performance figures represented a bit of a comedown!

Right: A tricycle front end was available for export territories.

Photographs on opposite page:

Top: The TVO model was not popular and a number were converted to diesel using the Perkins L4 engine.

Bottom: A 1953 Fordson Major diesel with oversize tyres.

Continuous Development

Numerous modifications were made to the engine in the years between 1952 and 1956, but it was in 1957 that the engine was updated, from tractor number 1425097 in April of that year. This had the effect of giving more power. The interesting thing is that the tractors so fitted were not advertised.

To confuse the issue, an industrial engine had been available from early 1957 with a modified manifold which allowed engine speed to peak at 1,800rpm. This was carried over onto the Mark II engines from 1425097 onwards, but was not recommended for agricultural use. What was so amazing was that the Mark II engine was not generally advertised! At the same time the TVO model was quietly dropped. It had taken just five years to firmly establish the compression ignition engine as the main power plant for the Fordson tractor.

The main reason for modifying the engine was that the extra power was needed for the forthcoming introduction, in July 1958, of the Power Major. This was rated at 51.8bhp @ 1,600rpm. To effect the maximum increase in power, modifications were made to the fuel injection pump.

All Mark II and Power Major engines are easily identified by the manifolds, the ports on the later engine being in line, the earlier engine having staggered ports. Indeed, the engine as fitted to the Power Major was to remain the same until June 1962, when the fitment of the Simms Minimec pump and mechanical governor raised the bhp to 53.7.

The Power Major also differed from the New Major in several other ways. The live PTO option had in fact come in with the New Major, from tractor No 1417988 in February 1957, but the main alterations to the new model apart from the engine output centred around a higher driving position with the instrument panel below the steering column. The throttle lever was moved. It was now located in a more convenient position below the steering column. New style wheel centres were also featured.

Details of the New Fordson Major with and without hydraulic lift and also showing the instrumentation.

*Above: The Fordson Dexta,
this is a post 1960 example,
with inset headlamps.*

*Left: The TVO engined New
Majors were only produced
until 1957.*

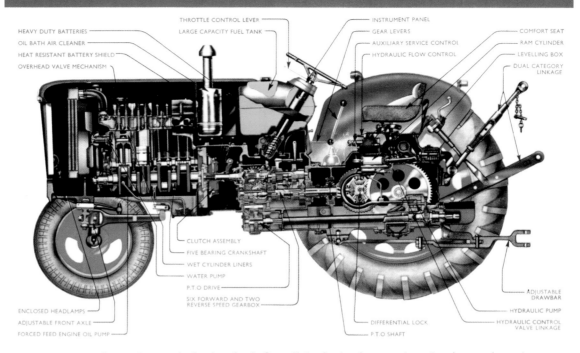

HEAVY DUTY BATTERIES
OIL BATH AIR CLEANER
HEAT RESISTANT BATTERY SHIELD
OVERHEAD VALVE MECHANISM

THROTTLE CONTROL LEVER
LARGE CAPACITY FUEL TANK

INSTRUMENT PANEL
GEAR LEVERS
AUXILIARY SERVICE CONTROL
HYDRAULIC FLOW CONTROL

COMFORT SEAT
RAM CYLINDER
LEVELLING BOX
DUAL CATEGORY LINKAGE

CLUTCH ASSEMBLY
FIVE BEARING CRANKSHAFT
WET CYLINDER LINERS
WATER PUMP
P.T.O DRIVE
SIX FORWARD AND TWO REVERSE SPEED GEARBOX

ENCLOSED HEADLAMPS
ADJUSTABLE FRONT AXLE
FORCED FEED ENGINE OIL PUMP

DIFFERENTIAL LOCK
P.T.O SHAFT

ADJUSTABLE DRAWBAR
HYDRAULIC PUMP
HYDRAULIC CONTROL VALVE LINKAGE

Extracts from a sales brochure for the Super Major showing the tractor in section above, and a service van of the period, below.

BLUE IS FOR
FORDSON FARMING VALUE

A Smaller Tractor

We need now to return to the age-old problem facing the Ford sales team, the 'Grey Menace'. No matter how successful the New Major was, the market for a smaller tractor was still, in the mid fifties, a wholly Ferguson preserve. Ford in the USA had concentrated, with considerable success, on this end of the market starting with the 8N which was in essence, an improved Ford Ferguson. Circumstances dictated that, in order to get out of the legal difficulties over the Ferguson patents, the very successful 8N Dearborn tractor which after all accounted for over 400,000 units in its four year run, had to be replaced. Indeed, the very fact that Ferguson's own Detroit line only built 140,000 units over the same period shows just how Ford could always beat the rest hands down.

The 8N was never available in the United Kingdom, although some got into southern Ireland, as did its replacement, the NAA. Indeed that model, produced for the jubilee of Ford, featured an engine driven hydraulic pump and other details which even the British built equivalent, when it arrived, did not have.

As we have observed earlier in this chapter, by far the most expensive item to develop for any tractor is the engine. Now the very engine which Ford was using in the 1950s was a non stressed unit also used on trucks of the period. When this was put into a tractor, it required a sub frame for additional strength. Ideally, a three cylinder version of this engine, modified in the same way in which Nuffield created the Universal Three out of the Universal Four, would have been ideal. But what would you have finished up with? Quite simply a derated diesel Major, possibly with smaller wheels and tyres, and a complete lack of the very features which made the Ferguson so popular. It would have been very attractive from the parts and service angle but not from the sales one.

The Fordson Dexta was restyled to match the Super Major on its introduction in 1960.

The Fordson Dexta used a version of the Perkins three cylinder diesel specially developed for Ford.

Ernest Doe's Dual Power used two Fordson Majors joined together to give a 100hp unit.

If Ford were going to successfully compete at this end of the market, their tractor had to be a Fergie look alike. This would involve the use of a stressed engine so that the unit construction could be maintained, and a high beam type front axle with dual track rod steering. The weight of a reduced Major in relation to a machine derived from an 8N based machine would also be at a dis-

advantage. How then could Ford enter the light end of the market without prohibitive investment in a new engine plant?

The involvement of Frank Perkins Ltd of Peterborough with Ford had been established solidly in the early postwar years when the P6 engine had been adopted for use in the E27N tractor and the Ford Thames Truck.

Perkins had available a P3 engine which was already being marketed as a conversion for the Ford 9N, 9NAN, 2N, 2NAN and 8N tractors. The fact that this engine was not available at the time when Ferguson was looking for a diesel engine for their TE-20 was unfortunate. The engine ultimately offered in this machine, the result of design consultation with Freeman Sanders, produced a power unit which would not start in anything but ambient temperatures. This left the market wide open for a Fergie sized tractor with an engine that would start!

As for the rest of the tractor, the basic design was based on the 8N but the gearbox was redesigned to give six forward speeds and two reverse. The move towards the provision of a live PTO was also taken into account in designing the tractor and this ture was the same as that incorporated into the 8N and pre-empted its adoption by Ford on the E1A model. It was strange however that none of the ideas then being developed in the NAA series of tractors in the USA, such as an engine driven 'live' hydraulic pump, came to the British machine which was called the Dexta. Relations between the agricultural divisions of the American and British companies were rather distant at that time.

Styling was based on the E1A with the fuel tank removed from over the engine completely in the same style. Most of the bought-in parts came from British suppliers such as brakes from Girling, an air filter from AC and Lucas electrical components.

With the introduction of the Super Major in 1960, the Dexta was altered to give grille

soon became an option, allowing operation of both PTO driven implements and the hydraulic system when the tractor was stationary.

The hydraulics were however, improved, and a much better design of pump was provided along with a redesigned top cover incorporating a separate external service facility. The position control/Qualitrol fea-

mounted headlamps. Later the Super Dexta and New Performance Dexta featured Minimec mechanically governed injection pumps, a restyled bonnet line with a peaked front and Super Dexta embellishment. The Dexta line came to an end when the Dexta was replaced by the 2000 which had come through the US development of the 8N and the Super Dexta by the 3000.

The formidable Dual Power was later developed into the Doe Triple D.

A petrol engined Dexta had also been available for export, however it is interesting to note how the Standard 87mm petrol engine was adopted for this model. This came about because Perkins were not able at that time to offer a petrol version of the F3 engine at a reasonable cost. Massey-Ferguson had just bought over the Standard Motor Company's Banner Lane plant at Coventry and were engaged in negotiations to buy Perkins, so the use of Standard's own engines looked finite.

There had been an abortive attempt to build a Standard tractor along with a company called New Idea, but this too floundered through lack of suitable finance. In the end Standard looked for other outlets and sold engines to Allis Chalmers and Ford, although the odd 87mm petrol engine was supplied to Massey-Ferguson right through to the mid 1970s.

The petrol Dexta with the Standard engine was actually some 11cm longer than the diesel version. The opportunity was taken to use this extra length to provide some extra fuel capacity for the tractor. These tractors were for export and were only sold in Australia, New Zealand, Norway, Sweden and Denmark.

There were other variations on the Dexta. An industrial version was produced, and Roadless Traction provided a 4 wheel drive model. A narrow build was also marketed, whilst it was left to the French to produce a vineyard type.

A New Fordson Major fitted with Perkins L4(TA) engine and County full tracks.

Left: A New Fordson Major equipped with experimental Dowty hydraulic transmission.

Below: Leeford Rotaped Tracks fitted to the New Fordson Major.

Above: A front mounted Whitlock Cultivator fitted to a New Fordson Major.

Below: This experimental NIAE hydrostatic tractor used the Fordson Major engine and other parts.

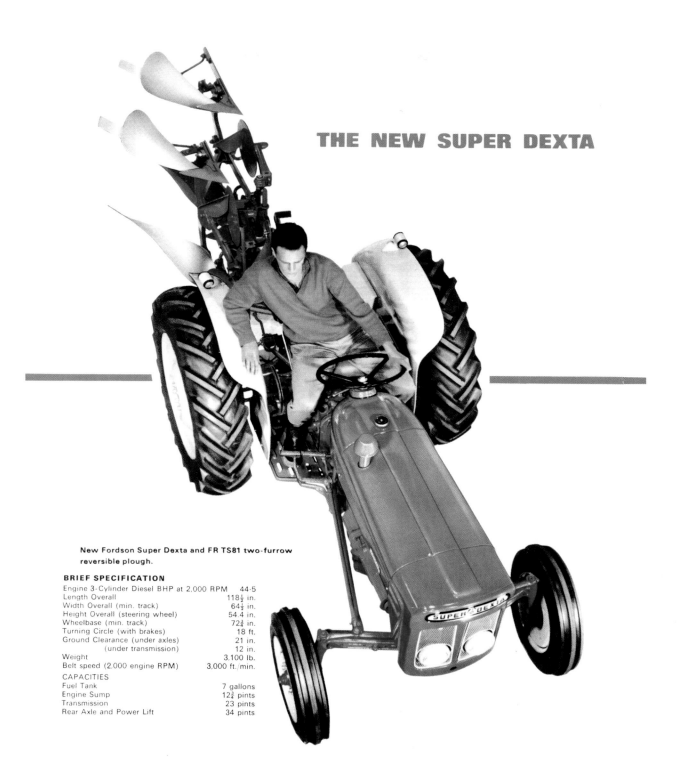

THE NEW SUPER DEXTA

New Fordson Super Dexta and FR TS81 two-furrow reversible plough.

BRIEF SPECIFICATION

Engine 3-Cylinder Diesel BHP at 2,000 RPM	44·5
Length Overall	$118\frac{1}{2}$ in.
Width Overall (min. track)	$64\frac{1}{2}$ in.
Height Overall (steering wheel)	54.4 in.
Wheelbase (min. track)	$72\frac{3}{4}$ in.
Turning Circle (with brakes)	18 ft.
Ground Clearance (under axles)	21 in.
(under transmission)	12 in.
Weight	3.100 lb.
Belt speed (2,000 engine RPM)	3,000 ft./min.

CAPACITIES

Fuel Tank	7 gallons
Engine Sump	$12\frac{3}{4}$ pints
Transmission	23 pints
Rear Axle and Power Lift	34 pints

The Super Dexta in its final blue/grey form after June 1963.

New Fordson Super Major.

NEW SUPER MAJOR WITH SUPER POWER

★ Engine power increased to 53.7 bhp.

★ A 30% increase in PTO power—now 42.5 hp at 540 rpm at the PTO, enough for the toughest jobs and always something in reserve.

★ New speed range—full pulling power available at speeds down to 1½ mph

★ New hydraulics with double-acting top link. More sensitive control means better transfer of power into work.

★ New Dual Flow Control gives adjustable lifting and lowering rates. New relief valve sustains maximum lifting power.

★ New 'Rest-O-Ride' seat, with adjustable suspension (optional).

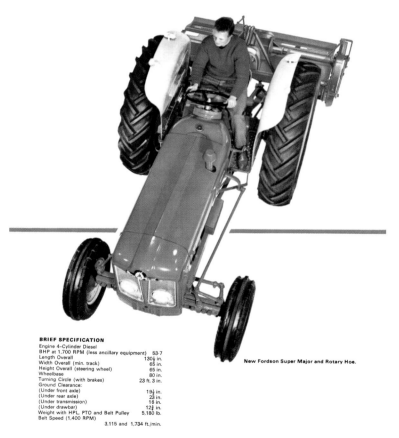

New Fordson Super Major and Rotary Hoe.

BRIEF SPECIFICATION
Engine 4-Cylinder Diesel
BHP at 1,700 RPM (less ancillary equipment)	53·7
Length Overall	130½ in.
Width Overall (min. track)	65 in.
Height Overall (steering wheel)	65 in.
Wheelbase	80 in.
Turning Circle (with brakes)	23 ft. 3 in.
Ground Clearance:	
(Under front axle)	19½ in.
(Under rear axle)	23 in.
(Under transmission)	16 in.
(Under drawbar)	12½ in.
Weight with HPL, PTO and Belt Pulley	5,180 lb.
Belt Speed (1,400 RPM)	
	3,115 and 1,734 ft./min.

The Super Major

We now must move out of the smaller end of the market to resume the story of the Fordson Major. The Power Major had the shortest life span of any model built at Dagenham. In 1960 a revised model was unveiled at the Smithfield show, Britain's premier agricultural event.

In fact, the first Super Major was built on 24th October of that year. The engine was virtually identical to that used in the Power Major. The main differences affected the transmission and hydraulics. The demand for extra grip to cope with the handling of heavier implements now coming into vogue saw the fitting of a differential lock; and instead of the faithful old dual shoe self energising slewing brakes inherited from the E27N, disc units were now employed, back in the original brake location hard against the transmission housing. On previous New Majors and Power Majors, bull pinion extensions were provided to minimise oil leakage. The designers now put their trust in current oilseal technology.

United Kingdom patents on the Ferguson draft control had expired for some time before they were applied to the Major. The Super Major featured a new hydraulic unit with draft control. Ford called their system, Position Control/ Qualitrol. At last the Ferguson draft control was breaking out of its designers, insistence on its application to light tractors only, and the robust unit fitted to the Super retained the same characteristics of its predecessor, with the improved design gear type hydraulic pump driven from the PTO shaft and drawing its oil supply from the rear transmission. The introduction of universal oils aided the operation of the unit considerably, especially in low ambient temperatures.

The appearance of the Super was further changed by the fitting of the headlamps within the two front grille panels, although this configuration only appeared on domestic agricultural models. The old side mounted lights plus a new style of front grille panel with pressed reinforcement bars was used on some export and industrial units.

In the world of diesel engines there was a general move away from pneumatic governing, and from April 1962 Fordson Major engines featured the Simms Minimec fuel injection pump with a mechanical governor built in as an extension of the pump body.

The New Performance Range

By June 1963 work was well advanced on the integration of all Ford tractor designs to produce the Worldwide range. The engine plant at Dagenham which produced the four and six-cylinder engines for trucks and tractors was reaching the end of its economic life. In any case, it was intended to move tractor production in 1964 to the new Basildon operation.

Nevertheless, tractor production had to be maintained and models still updated to satisfy an expanding market. The Super Major was given its last face-lift and with some modifications to the engine in the

Illustration on opposite page:

June 1963 saw the New Fordson Super Major launched.

Above: After production of the Super Major ceased at Dagenham, the tractor continued to be built in Spain.

Right: Details of a Power Major which was in essence a halfway house between the New Major and Super Major models.

area of the camshaft and valves, gave a greater output at 53.7bhp. One of the inherent weaknesses with the Fordson Major was its rather poor ground speed PTO capability, and this saw gear ratios altered to improve performance when running with PTO driven implements, such as a pick-up baler.

To lessen the shock when new models were to arrive, the New Performance Super Major was finished in a new blue and grey colour scheme. Bonnet badges gave way to stickers and the hydraulics were also improved by the addition of a flow control to enable the rate of lowering to be adjusted, a great aid with the heavier reversible ploughs now appearing.

This was not the end of the story as far as the tractor was concerned. The Ebro organisation in Spain had been set up by Ford to build vehicles in the 1950s. Ford later relinquished control of Ebro to the Spanish government, but in 1964/5 the tooling and production facilities were transferred to Spain to allow production of the E1A model to be started there under licence. Attempts were later made to sell the Ebro 160E in the United Kingdom and some hybrid models were built using Perkins engines and the old Super Major transmission. Latterly Ford bought quite a few spares from Ebro for the E1A range.

Above: Power Major with tricycle conversion. Note the lack of hydraulic lift.

Below: The Super Major was sold in the USA as the Ford 5000 Diesel.

Above: This petrol engined
Dexta used a Standard Motor
Company engine.

Left: A New Major as supplied
to Australia.

AMERICAN DEVELOPMENTS 1952-1963

Right: The Ford Jubilee tractor as first introduced in 1952.

Below: A rear view of the Jubilee NAA. The live hydraulics were powered by an engine driven pump.

As we have seen earlier, the relationship between Ferguson and Ford in the USA, which had begun with a handshake, ended in an acrimonious lawsuit. The settlement of this provided that the 8N tractor, which incorporated Ferguson's draft control, should be withdrawn from production by 1952. Ironically, by the time the new model to replace the 8N was ready, the patents covering certain features of Ferguson's hydraulic system had actually expired in the USA.

Jubilee

The 1953 NAA or Jubilee tractor as it was called, retained many of the features of the 8N, but a completely new engine was provided. Dubbed the Red Tiger, it was an overhead valve unit of 134 cu in with a bore of 3.4375in and a stroke of 3.6in. A new feature was the engine driven hydraulic pump which gave live hydraulics. Dry liners were employed in the cylinder block, and rotator exhaust valves. A single plate 9in clutch drove a four speed constant mesh gearbox.

All subsequent American Ford models were based on the NAA. The use of model numbers to indicate differences in specification may give the impression that there was a vast range of different tractors available. In fact there was one basic design which was developed over the next ten years to give a whole selection of variants.

The first additions to the range came in 1955 when the 600 and 800 series were introduced. The 600 series was basically an updated NAA with the same engine, indeed the 640 was nothing more than that tractor with badge changes. The 650 however was provided with an extra forward gear, and a single 10in clutch.

The 660 also had the five speed gearbox, and featured a double 9in clutch and a live PTO. The 850 had the same basic features as the 650, but the 172 cu in engine with 3.9in bore and 3.6in stroke gave more power. The 860 enjoyed the same features as the 660, but with a bigger engine.

More Variations

The next update to these models came in late 1957, when the 640 became the 641, the 650 the 651 and the 660 the 661. The 600 series was dubbed the Workmaster and the red paint was extended to cover the bonnet. In addition two utility models were added to the 600 range, the 621 without many of the extras and no hydraulics and the 631 with hydraulics. The utility models, the 621 and 631, retained the four speed gearbox.

The most interesting development was the addition of a rowcrop model to the

The Ford Jubilee tractors, the example seen here dates from 1954, formed the basis of an extended range from 1955.

69

range. The 741 featured the addition of a subframe to the sides and front of the engine, which enabled a wide front axle, single front or vee twin wheels to be fitted. Ground clearance was raised by the fitting of reduction housings to the ends of the rear axle shafts.

The 800 series was dubbed the Powermaster and the 841, with only four forward speeds, was added to the range. The 850 became the 851 and the 860 the 861. An 821 utility model was added to the range with no hydraulics or extras. The rowcrop version was the 951 with a single clutch, and the 961 had a dual clutch and live PTO.

To add to the variety of models available, diesel engines were introduced in 1958, though at first only on the 800 series. The engine was a development of the gasoline 172 cu in unit. At the same time the four speed transmission variants, the 841, 941, and 821, were made available with an optional auxiliary transmission providing

70

12 forward speeds. It was not long before the 600 series was offered with the option of a diesel engine as well, a 144 cu in unit being provided.

Select-0-Speed

Select-0-Speed was the next complication in adding to the variants available. This was a shift on the move transmission giving ten forward and two reverse speeds. The 621 with SOS became the 611, the 641 the 671, the 741 the 771, the 661 the 681, the 821 the 811, the 851 the 871, the 861 the 881, the 951 the 971 and the 961 the 981. If readers find all these variants confusing, the explanatory information on page 77 will hopefully clarify matters.

Liquid petroleum gas was all the rage in the USA as a fuel in the fifties and needless to say all the Fords were available with the capability of using this form of fuel. It only remains now to cover the offset models, which were based on the rowcrop. By fitting an offset front axle, modified steering, and short and long half shaft housings, the 741 rowcrop became the 541 offset.

The 801 Powermaster featured the larger engine.

A US built Ford 3000. Petrol engines were still very popular in the United States at this time.

Red To Blue

In 1962, as a step towards consolidation now that the new Worldwide series was on the horizon, the whole range was updated and reliveried. There were now only two basic designations, the 4000 range which encompassed the 172 cu in engined models, and the 2000 range which encompassed the 134-144 cu in engined models. Livery was now all blue for the 2000 range, with grey fenders, and blue with a white bonnet and fenders for the 4000 range. All the same options as before were available.

A Big Ford Tractor In The USA

We now have to track back in time to cover the introduction of the largest model in the American Ford range. The Ford 6000 Commander was a tractor with many very advanced features. It was available with either a six cylinder 223 cu in gasoline or 242 cu in diesel engine. Select-O-Speed transmission was standard, along with an accumulator hydraulic system, power disc brakes and power adjusted rear wheels, and an adjustable steering column to allow operation whilst static. It was available in vee twin and standard wide axle forms, with power steering of course. New in a red and grey livery, it was reliveried in blue and white in 1962 and in 1964 the frontal styling was altered to match the new range. It was phased out in 1967. In many ways the Commander was ahead of its time, but valuable information gleaned from its operation helped in developing later models.

Worldwide Markets

In the beginning, there was but one Fordson tractor, the parent of all unit construction tractors from many manufacturers worldwide, the Fordson Model F.

The motor industry, even in the mid 1960s, was undergoing big changes. The forward looking companies, not subsidised by governments, foresaw the creation of a

The Ford 6000 Commander.

range of vehicles which could be marketed worldwide, and built around the globe in different locations, interdependent on each other for certain components, which by virtue of economies of scale, could be produced at much lower unit costs.

Ford in the UK was repossessed by the parent US concern in 1963, and as space at Dagenham was needed for other projects, tractor production was devolved to a new division. A new plant built at Basildon in Essex, not far from Dagenham, which, with two others at Detroit in the USA and in Belgium, would construct a new range of tractors common in most respects for all territories, but with options to suit requirements in both the eastern and western hemispheres. These tractors used many components made in the three plants in Britain, Belgium and the USA.

It might also be added here that the old Dagenham range was very popular in the USA. Fordson Super Majors, Dextas, and Super Dextas were sold there in numbers,

latterly being finished in special paint schemes for the US market. The Super Dexta was sold as the Ford Diesel 2000 and the New Super Major as the Ford Diesel 5000, from 1962 to 1964. American users speak highly of the Dagenham built machines even today. 1964 saw the completion of the Basildon plant and the stage was set to introduce the new models worldwide.

The smallest tractor in the new range, known collectively as the 6x series, was the 2000. Following experience with the three cylinder Dexta engine, it had a three cylinder diesel engine with a bhp of 37 @ 2000 rpm.

Six forward speeds were provided, along with a transmission PTO (live PTO was optional), and independent hydraulics. Shoe type steering brakes were provided. The engine had a bore and stroke of 4.2 x 3.8 in and a petrol version was produced, the three cylinder engine being a derivative of the diesel design and not related to any

A comparison between the first Fordson production line at Dearborn and the new Basildon production facility when opened in 1964.

Another batch of new Ford tractors leaves the Basildon plant by rail.

previous US engines. The new tractors were finished in blue with grey wheels.

The next model in the range was the 3000. Its engine, with its 4.2in bore and stroke, produced 47bhp and made use of the same block as the 2000 but with a greater stroke, a technique used also in the Ford Motor Company's car engines.

The PTO on the 3000 was an independent unit with its own clutch operated hydraulically and the hydraulic system had a greater pump output than the 2000. Main dimensions were similar to the 2000 and various alternative wheel and tyre sizes were available. An eight speed gearbox was provided.

The 4000 was equipped with a three cylinder 56bhp engine with a 4.4in bore and stroke. Eight forward speeds plus independent PTO were standard and totally enclosed disc brakes were provided inside the rear axle shafts. A petrol engined version was also available.

The 5000 or Super Major was the largest of the new range. It started life with a four cylinder engine of 4.4in bore by 4.2in stroke and this unit developed 67bhp @ 2,000rpm. Eight speeds were available from the gearbox, although like the other models of the period, Select-O-Speed was available.

For sale in the western hemisphere row-crop, vee twin and wide front axle variants were available.

It took just over three years in worldwide service for teething problems to be resolved. By 1968 the Ford force was with us, with all four models being given improved specifications. There was an increase in engine power on the larger models, the 4000 going up from 56 to 62bhp, and the 5000 going up from 67 to 75bhp. In addition the PTO speed on the 5000 was increased by 20%. Improvements to the engines of all models included a new cylinder head, heavier connecting rods and high lift camshafts. An improved clutch and redesigned selector mechanisms made gear changing easier. On the larger models, the 4000 and 5000, the front axle mounting was improved. New round silencers were fitted in place of the oval units of the early models.

Along with these improvements came a restyle with a squared up front ends and full length bonnet decals. In addition weather cabs were made available for the full tractor range.

Despite being over 40 years old, many Fordson Super Majors remain at work.

Serial Numbers

Model F produced Dearborn Michigan

1917	1	to	259
1918	260	to	34426
1919	34427	to	92113
1920	92114	to	169583
1921	169584	to	201025
1922	201026	to	268582
1923	268583	to	370351
1924	370352	to	455359
1925	455360	to	567607
1926	557608	to	629830
1927/8	629830	to	747681

Model F produced Cork

Cork numbers are in same series as Dearborn

1919	63001	to	63200
1920	65001	to	65500
	105001	to	108229
1921	108230	to	109672
1922	109673	to	110000
	170958	to	172000
	250001	to	250300
	253001	to	253562

Model N produced at Cork

1929	747682	to	757368
1930	757369	to	772564
1931	772565	to	776065

Model N transition from Cork to Dagenham

1932	776066	to	719135

The latter part of the above production came off the Dagenham line, many Cork parts were used until 1934.

Model N produced Dagenham

First tractor off the line in each year shown

1933	779154	1940	854238
1934	781967	1941	874914
1935	785548	1942	897624
1936	794703	1943	925274
1937	807581	1944	957574
1938	826779	1945	975419
1939	837826		

Last Model N No 983647, built 4th June 1945

First E27N No 980520 built on 19th March 1945

1945	980520	1949	1104657
1946	993489	1950	1138235
1947	1018978	1951	1180610
1948	1054094	1952	1216575

Last E27N built, No 1216990 on 17th January 1952

New Fordson Major

First E1A model produced 21st December 1951, No 1217101. Full production began, 1st January 1952 with No 1217104

1951	1217101	1955	1322546
1952	1217104	1956	1371418
1953	1247281	1957	1412429
1954	1276857	1958	1458394

Last New Fordson Major built, No 1481013 August 1958. Optional live PTO from No 1417988, 1957

Fordson Power Major

First built July 1958. Full production began, August 1958 with No 1481091

1958	1481091	1960	1537893
1959	1494458		

Last Power Major built 21st November 1960, No 1578885

Fordson Super Major

First built 24th October 1960, No 1575971. Full production began, 22nd November 1960 with No 1578886

1960	1575971	1961	1583906

New numbering introduced November 1961

1961		08 A 300001
1962		08 B 741001
1963	January	08 C 781470
1963	February	08 C 945000
1963	June	Blue/Grey
1964	January	08 D 945000
1964	September	08 D 976148

The latter was the last Dagenham built Fordson

Fordson Dexta

1958	January	957E/144
1959		957E/22558
1960		957E/44432
1961		957E/71921
1961	Nov	Diff lock standard
1962		09A/312001
1963	January	09C/732031

1963	February	09C/900001
1963	June	Blue/Grey
1964	January	O9D/900001
1964	September	O9D/928428

The latter was the last one built

Fordson Super Dexta

1962	April	09B/710530
1963	January	09B/731454
1963	February	09C/900001
1963	June	Blue/Grey
1964	January	O9D/900001
1964	September	O9D/928248

The latter was the last one built

US Built Ford Tractors

Ford 9N

Each serial number was prefixed by either 9N for petrol, 9NAN VO in the UK or 2N for a utility tractor on steel wheels.

1939	1-14643	1943	107755
1940	14644	1944	131783
1941	47843	1945	174638
1942	92363	1946	204129
1947	267289-306221		

Ford 8N

1947	1	1950	245637
1948	37908	1951	343593
1949	141370	1952	442035

The latter was the last one built. Serial numbers were stamped on left side of engine block.

Ford NAA.

1952	NAA - 1
1953	4930
1954	77478

All numbers were prefixed by the letters, NAA. This serial number was stamped on right side of the engine block up to No 22239 and on the transmission housing to the rear of starter motor thereafter.

Ford 600/700/800/900

1954	1	1956	77271
1955	10615	1957	116368

Ford 601/701/801/901

1957	1001
1960	106258
1958	11997
1961	131427
1959	58312
1962	155531

In the 600 to 901 series tractors, the serial number was stamped on top of the transmission housing at the left front corner. The serial number was prefixed by three or five digits to identify the model number.

In all post 1964 Ford tractors, the serial number was located on the off side transmission case and was in code. The number is made up of three components:
Prefix figure = last figure of year, eg 5 = 1965
Month letter = Jan-Dec, A to M
Day = date of production, 1 to 31.
For example, a Ford 3000 numbered 8E01 was built on 1st May 1968

Ford American Models 1955-62

The tractor model and serial numbers were stamped on the top of the transmission housing at the front left corner. A different model number was assigned to each major product option. Early agricultural and industrial model numbers consisted of three digits, followed in some cases by a suffix consisting of a number and/or letter. The first digit designated the engine size and tractor type, the second digit the transmission type and the third digit the year of the series. The following table lists the product options indicated by the model number.

First digit

5** - One row, 8in offset design equipped with 134cu.in gasoline or LPG or 144cu.in diesel engine.

6** - Four-wheel, adjustable axle design equipped with 134cu.in gasoline or LPG or 144cu.in diesel engine.

7** - High clearance row-crop type equipped with 134cu.in gasoline or LPG or 144cu.in diesel engine.

8** - Four-wheel, adjustable axle design equipped with 172cu.in engine.

9** - High clearance row-crop type equipped with 172cu.in engine.

18** - Four-wheel, axle type, industrial tractor equipped with 172cu.in engine.

Second digit

1 - Select-O-Speed transmission without PTO.

2 - Four-speed transmission without PTO or hydraulic lift.

3 - Four-speed transmission without PTO.

4 - Four-speed transmission.

5 - Five-speed transmission with transmission PTO.

6 - Five-speed transmission with live PTO.

7 - Select-O-Speed transmission with single speed PTO.

8 - Select-O-Speed transmission with two speed and ground drive PTO.

Third digit

**0 - Series designation built 1955 1958.

**1 - Series designation built 1958 1962.

Suffixes

***-1- Tricycle type with single front wheel.

***-4- High-clearance, four-wheel, adjustable axle type.

***-D- Diesel engine.

***-L- LPG engine.

***-37- Equipped with reversing transmission.

***-21- Equipped with combination transmission.

GLOSSARY

All Around – Name given to the rowcrop version of the Fordson sold in the USA.

Belt Horsepower – Power measured at the tractor's power delivery point. This is usually at a belt pulley attachment but can also be at the PTO (cf) bhp. See also horsepower.

Brake Horsepower (bhp) – The power developed by an engine under test when attached to a device which measures power under load.

Carcass – The basic tractor before wheels and tinwork were added. Casting codes figures, part of each casting pattern, enable the date of the casting to be ascertained.

Compression Ignition – An engine, such as a diesel, reliant on a high compression ratio to self ignite the fuel.

Compression Ratio – A measurement achieved by taking the volume of an engine cylinder when at bottom dead centre (at the bottom of its stroke) and at top dead centre (at the top of its stroke). By varying the size of the combustion chamber in the cylinder head, high compression can be achieved for fuels like petrol, and low compression for TVO or Lamp Oil.

Conversion Pack – An engine plus a kit of parts to allow a tractor to be converted to diesel.

Distillate – Similar product to TVO produced in North America.

Double Clutch – A clutch assembly with two driven plates, one to transmit power to the gearbox and the other to the power take off. See also live hydraulics.

Draft Control – The fundamental feature of the Ferguson System whereby a constant depth in work is maintained by the hydraulic system.

Drawbar Horsepower – . Power measured at the tractor drawbar on test.

Dry Liner – Where the engine cylinder block has the cylinders cast in and is sleeved.

E27N – The designation given to the Fordson Major built at Dagenham from 1945 to 1952

Eastern Hemisphere – The tractor sales area consisting of Europe and Asia.

Greenfield Village Museum – located near Detroit, Michigan, USA set up by Henry Ford to chart US engineering and social history.

Handshake Agreement – The name given to an accord between two or more persons where nothing is put in writing.

Horsepower – The power developed by an internal combustion engine calculated basically by the cubic capacity of the engine. See also drawbar horsepower, brake horsepower (bhp) and belt horsepower.

Lamp Oil – Ordinary Kerosine or Paraffin used in some territories as a tractor fuel.

Land Utility – The name given to the Fordson Model N and E27N tractors when fitted with low pressure pneumatic tyres.

Live Hydraulics – Where the drive to the hydraulic pump which operates the three point linkage is not broken when the tractor is stopped or put out of gear. This can be achieved by a double clutch (cf) or by driving the hydraulic pump direct from the engine.

LTX – The designation given to the big Ferguson prototypes of the early 1950s.

Magneto – Self contained device for generating high tension ignition current on an engine.

Mercury V8 – A widely used Ford car and truck engine of the 1930s.

Ministry of Supply – The body which controlled all industrial production in the UK during the 1939/45 war.

Model N – The designation letter given to the Standard Fordson produced from 1929-45.

NAA – Ford Jubilee tractor built from 1951 to avoid the use of Ferguson patents.

Plow – The American word for a plough. Also used to describe the number of furrows a tractor would be capable of pulling, for example, a two plow tractor.

Position Control – An added feature of Ford and later Fordson tractors whereby the draft control could be locked and an implement held at fixed depth.

Pressure Lubrication – The forcing of oil into components of a vehicle engine by means of a pump.

Proprietory – Name given to an accessory produced for a motor vehicle by a company other than the manufacturer of the vehicle.

PSV – Public Service Vehicle, a British designation, for a bus, tram or trolleybus.

PTO – Power take off. A splined shaft at the rear of the tractor used to power implements. by means of a shaft fitted with universal couplings.

Row Crop – A tractor with adjustable track front and rear or with single or vee front wheel configuration suitable for row crop cultivation.

Spark Ignition – An engine reliant on an electric spark to ignite the fuel.

Standard Agricultural – The name given by Ford to the basic Fordson tractor on steel wheels with either cleats or spade lugs as an option on the rear rims.

Sump – The base of an internal combustion engine usually used to contain the lubricant.

Three Point Linkage – The essential feature of the Ferguson system whereby the implement is attached to the tractor by one top link and two lower links. It was used by Fordson without the draft control from 1946-57.

Torque Convertor – Means of transmitting power from the engine to the rear wheels hydraulically.

TVO, Tractor Vaporising Oil – A hybrid fuel produced during the distillation of crude oil which is not volatile enough to attract excise duty. Specifically produced for agricultural use it had additives to bring its octane value up to around 60.

Vaporiser – Device for preheating low cost fuels (see TVO, Lamp Oil, Distillate) to allow for efficient combustion in an internal combustion engine.

Vineyard Model – A tractor with narrow track to fit between cultivations such as grape vines, hops or berries.

War Agricultural Committees – The county based bodies which oversaw food production in the United Kingdom during the 1939-45 war. They also licenced the purchase of tractors.

Western Hemisphere – The tractor sales area consisting of the Americas.

Wet liner – Where the engine cylinder bores are separate from the block and fitted with suitable seals.

FURTHER READING

Classic Farm Tractors
Cletus Hohman
Voyageur Press

Ford Farm Tractors
Randy Leffingwell
MBI Publishing Company

Ford N Series Tractors
Rod Beemer and Chester Peterson Jr
MBI Publishing Company

**The Ford Tractor Story
Part 1 Dearborn To Dagenham**
Stuart Gibbard
Japonica Press

Great Tractor Builders Ferguson
Allan T Condie
Ian Allan Publishing

Vintage Ford Tractors
Rober N Pripps
Voyageur Press

**Vintage Tractor Special 4, Fordson Ns
1929-45**
Allan T. Condie
Allan T. Condie Publications.

**Vintage Tractor Special 5, Fordson
E27Ns 1945-52**
Allan T. Condie
Allan T. Condie Publications.

**Vintage Tractor Special 9, American
Fordson & Ford 1917-1970**
Allan T. Condie
Allan T. Condie Publications.

**Vintage Tractor Special 10, New
Fordson Major E1As 1952-64**
Allan T. Condie
Allan T. Condie Publications.

**Vintage Tractor Special 11, Fordson
Model N Miscellany 1929-45**
Allan T. Condie
Allan T. Condie Publications.